The Frog Princess

Written by Lisa Thompson

Pictures by Andy Hamilton

The Princess wanted a pet to play with.

The Prince gave her a frog.

"Frogs are not fun,"
said the Princess.

"This frog is different,"
said the Prince.

"Let's see who can swim the fastest," said the frog to the Princess.

"Too easy," said the Princess.

She raced the frog around the moat and won.

"Let's see who can jump the highest," said the frog.

"Too easy," said the Princess.

She jumped twice as high as the frog and won.

"Let's see who can catch the most flies," said the frog.

"Too easy," said the Princess.

She grabbed her brother's flycatcher.

She caught more flies than the frog and won.

"What do you want to do next?" asked the frog.

FLY PAPER

"Let's see who can croak the loudest," said the Princess.

"Too easy," said the frog.

The Princess opened her mouth to croak.

The frog leapt over and gave her a big kiss.

13

The Princess turned into a frog.

"Reeeedeeeeeep!" croaked the frog as loudly as he could to his new frog Princess.

"I won," said the frog.

What did the Princess do better than the frog?

How did the frog win in the end?

How do you think the Princess felt when she turned into a frog?